"SAVE ME JESUS"

KENNETH E. SOLA JR.

———*ᴄᴠᴠᴏ*———

John 3:27: "John answered and said, 'A man can receive nothing unless it has been given to him from heaven.'"

Come, Holy Spirit, use my mouth to speak Your words.

In Jesus' name.

Take everything I say with a grain of salt and chew on it,

For this is not milk, this is the meat of the Word

And the Bread of Life

People, we are dining in the throne room.

Brother Ken

Deuteronomy 8:3: "So He humbled you, allowed you to hunger, and fed you with manna which you did not know, nor your fathers know, that He might make you know that man shall not live by bread alone; but man lives by every word that proceeds from the mouth of the Lord."

John 4:32: "But He said to them, 'I have food to eat of which you do not know.' Therefore the disciples said to one another, 'Has anyone brought Him anything to eat?' Jesus said to them, 'My food is to do the will of Him who sent Me, and to finish His work.'"

Luke 8:8: "'But others fell on good ground, sprang up, and yielded a crop of a hundredfold.' When He had said these things He cried, 'He who has ears to hear, let him hear!'"

—*∾*—

Hello, my name is Ken Sola. On Wednesday, January 16th, 2013, I received a vision from GOD, and I would like to share. The vision was my day in court on Judgment Day and the surprising ending. Now, put that on the back burner of your mind.

I'm forty-five and was born in Baltimore, Maryland in 1967. I grew up running the shorelines of the lower Potomac River and Chesapeake Bay in southern Maryland. I had the usual protestant Christian upbringing: baptized, christened, confirmed, Sunday school, vacation bible school.

When I was twenty-five, a man showed me in the Bible that where John chapter three starts off, there was a "man of the Pharisees named Nicodemus, a ruler of the Jews. This man came to Jesus by night and said to Him,

'Rabbi, we know that You are a teacher come from God; for no one can do these signs that You do unless God is with him'" (John 3:1-2). John 3:3 continues:

> Jesus answered and said to him, "Most assuredly, I say to you, unless one is born again, he cannot see the kingdom of God." Nicodemus said to Him, "How can a man be born when he is old? Can he enter a second time into his mother's womb and be born?" Jesus answered, "Most assuredly, I say to you, unless one is born of water and the Spirit, he cannot enter the kingdom of God. That which is born of the flesh is flesh, and that which is born of the Spirit is spirit."

Now doctors say that the human body is 97% water, so I think our physical birth is the water birth. Now what about the spiritual birth? Well, Romans 10:9 says that if you "confess with your mouth the Lord Jesus and believe in your heart that God has raised Him from the dead, you will be saved." What does this mean? To be born again spiritually, we must each pray out loud, "SAVE ME JESUS!"

So I prayed, "save me, Jesus," and was born again spiritually.

Therefore, if anyone is in Christ, he is a new creation; old things have passed away; behold, all things have become new. 2 Corinthians 5:17

Was there a parade? Or were there trumpets sounding? Maybe in Heaven, but I had to go back to work. Everything still seemed the same, but church was better. It was warm, I was home, and the people were nice, too.

I had only been saved about a year or two when I learned that I am an evangelist. Well, being overjoyed and in love with Jesus, I said, "I need to save the world for Jesus!" Now, I can't even save money, so I know it's not me doing the saving; it's Jesus. My "Great Commission" is this: "Go therefore and make disciples of all the nations, baptizing them in the name of the Father and of the Son and of the Holy Spirit" (Matt 28:19).

Why me? Why did God show me this vision? I don't know; I stopped asking why. All I do know is that I'm on a mission from God!

People, I'm not pretty. I've been arrested ten times. In 1988, I wrecked my car and was in a coma for five weeks. They threw me out of the Marine Corps! YOU WANT TO FIGHT? JOIN the MARINES! Those boys threw me out! It was all right though: I got an honorable disregard and a hat. They say, "once a Marine..." On June 4 1986, President Ronald Regan was the guest speaker at my graduation from Parris Island.

I guess I hit rock bottom sometime around 2010. I was divorced, homeless and it was against the law for me to see my children. (My ex-wife had a restraining order against me.) Things were bad—as usual—and getting worse. I remember praying, "God, I can't believe life is supposed to be this hard. What's going on?"

It was during the last police investigation. I won't go into details; let's just say it was worse than usual. My thirty-five-hundred-dollar lawyer said I could be looking at thirty years in jail. Where does this stuff come from?!

I'm tired... I don't want to do this anymore.

Have you ever cussed at God?

When I knew, that I knew, that I could not commit suicide...

Fortunately:

Romans 8:35 says: "Who shall separate us from the love of Christ. Shall tribulation or distress or persecution, or famine, or nakedness, or peril, or sword?"

Romans 8:38 says: "For I am persuaded that neither death nor life, nor angels nor principalities nor powers, nor things present nor things to come, nor height nor depth, nor any other created thing, shall be able to separate us from the love of God which is in Christ Jesus our Lord."

Hebrews 13:5 says: "Let your conduct be without covetousness; be content with such things as you have. For He Himself said, 'I will never leave you or forsake you.'"

What can separate me from the Love of God? Nothing!

I CHECKED!

Well, if that's no longer an option, now what do I do? I guess I have to go back to work, again. That's all I had: my job and my truck. When there's nothing left, all you have is prayer.

9

2 Corinthians 12:9 says: "And He said to me, 'My grace is sufficient for you, for My strength is made perfect in weakness.'"

I heard Reverend Jesse Jackson say, "PUSH: Pray Until Something Happens." I heard Bishop Taffi Dollar say, "We've got to fight!" I said, "I've been fighting all my life and I've got nothing!" I heard the Holy Ghost say, "Fight smart, not hard."

I'm coming up out of here!

I put all that Bible stuff to the test. Everyday I prayed an angelic hedgerow of protection around me and those who were mine. I pleaded the blood of Jesus over me and my family. I assigned angels around all of us, to protect us physically, emotionally and spiritually, in Jesus' name.

I started claiming everything I could find in the Bible:

You pushed me violently, that I might fall, but the Lord helped me. The Lord is my strength and my song, and He has become my salvation. Psalm 118:13

This is the day the Lord has made; I will rejoice and be glad in it. Psalm 118:24

And one seraphim cried to another and said: "Holy, holy, holy is the Lord of hosts; the whole earth is full of His glory!" Isaiah 6:3

But seek first the kingdom of God and His righteousness, and all these things will be added to you. Matthew 6:33

For every beast of the forest is Mine, and the cattle on a thousand hills. Psalm 50:10

So shall My word be that goes forth from My mouth; it shall not return to Me void, but it shall accomplish what I please, and it shall prosper in the thing for which I sent it. Isaiah 55:11

If all I've got is this job, I'm going to work it. In 2011, I made $15,000 in overtime pay. In 2012 I made $23,000 in overtime. Who knows what this year will look like? Now, is it all about the money? No, but everything else is!

In January of 2013, I heard Bishop Creflo Dollar say that there has been some kind of a shift in the spirit world. I didn't know what happened or what that meant, but I started thinking back, because things have been getting better lately. I was homeless until April of 2012 when I saw Big Brother Steve Hagen, Master Sergeant USMC (ret). He asked, "What's up?" I told him, "Life's been kicking my behind." He said, "You can crash." In October of 2012, I got good news when I made an appointment to donate blood. The lady congratulated me, because my November donation brought my donation total to five gallons. Give blood; Jesus did!

The second week in December, I put stickers on the front of my truck that said, "save me Jesus". I've known for a long time that I'm an evangelist and I haven't been a very good witness lately. I thought of the "save me Jesus" sign about two years ago, and bought the stickers about then. I kept talking myself out of putting them on my truck. "Oh, I need help to get them on straight; oh I can't say that, that's crazy!" The second week in December, I went ahead and put them on.

Then, later in December, I worked thirteen days straight, which I've never done before, and that's good since I live off of overtime pay. Working thirteen days in a row, two weeks before the year 2013 made me wonder, also. This is going to be a good year! Things are getting better.

—⟨∿∿⟩—

I t took three days to receive this vision, and I didn't know I was receiving a vision.

Monday, January 14: it was raining. I work at an airport. Not much was happening that day. Tuesday, the same thing. It was slow around the office. Wednesday, more of the same. I've got a lot on my mind. I had gotten a piece of the vision each day, and not realized it. Wednesday afternoon or evening (I'm not sure), "POW!" It hit me. In my minds eye, I saw three big pieces of a round puzzle fall into place and then the whole thing came into focus. I didn't realize until months later that the picture on the round puzzle was a picture of the earth from outer space.

Picture in your mind's eye a television court show. There were only four of us in the room. Now it was like a dream, everything was in the shadows. I could tell the

Judge was up on His bench, but all I could see was a black silhouette of the back of His chair. Jesus—Judge, Advocate, Good Counselor—was sitting at the table to my left. Standing at the table to my right was Satan, accuser of the brethren. After Satan got done accusing me (my sin life did not flash before my eyes, I just knew he was done) he said, "If that's not bad enough, he's a sorry sack of sin-and-something."

Everything was quiet. I looked to my left to see what Jesus was going to say. Jesus was a stone statue! His arms were folded on His chest! Then, from the shadow on the bench:

"WELL DONE, MY GOOD AND FAITHFUL SERVANT,

YOU LOOK LIKE MY SON JESUS IN THAT SUIT

OF RIGHTOUSNESS."

End of vision

I will greatly rejoice in the Lord, my soul shall
be joyful in my God; for He has clothed me with
garments of salvation, He has covered me with
the robe of righteousness, as a bridegroom decks

15

himself with ornaments, and as a bride adorns herself with her jewels. Isaiah 61:10

For you are all sons of God through faith in Christ Jesus. For as many of you as were baptized into Christ have put on Christ. Galatians 3:26

Does the biblical-era outer garment of a "robe of righteousness" translate to a modern-day outer garment of a suit of righteousness? Or did the church body get a makeover?

During the vision, I realized all of our sins are recorded in Heaven. By the devil, not by God! God always has been and always will be (Rom. 1:20). He knows the end from the beginning (Ecc. 3:11). He counted the cost (Rom. 4:5). The price was paid on the cross at Calvary. By the atoning sacrifice of the blood of the lamb of God, that was slain before the foundations of the world, "being justified freely by His grace through the redemption that is in Christ Jesus, whom God set forth as a propitiation by His blood, through faith, to demonstrate His righteousness, because in His forbearance God had passed over the sins that were previously committed, to demonstrate at this time His righteousness, that He might be just and the justifier of the one who has faith in Jesus" (Rom. 3:24).

As you can imagine, I was bouncing off the walls. I got a vision! Well done, my good and faithful! Oh, wow! Dude! I got a vision! I knew this vision was for every member of the church body.

This is when I realized we are all in constant prayer. How can this be; doesn't the human body need sleep? Well, I have had dreams from the Lord, too, and that wasn't my fault either.

> The Spirit of truth, whom the world cannot receive, because it neither sees Him nor knows Him; but you know Him, for He dwells with you and will be in you. John 14:17

> Jesus answered and said to him, "If anyone loves Me, he will keep My word; and My Father will love him, and we will come to him and make our home with him." John 14:23

17

In Him you also trusted, after you heard the word of truth, the gospel of your salvation; in whom also, having believed, you were sealed with the Holy Spirit of promise, who is the guarantee of our inheritance until the redemption of the purchased possession, to the praise of His glory. Ephesians 1:14

But if the Spirit of Him who raised Jesus from the dead dwells in you, He who raised Christ from the dead will also give life to your mortal bodies through His Spirit who dwells in you. Romans 8:11

For your Father knows the things you have need of before you ask Him. Matthew 6:8

We pray with our thoughts and words. If you don't hear the Lord, ask Him to teach you. Try this: in your mind pray silently, "Holy Spirit can you hear me, because I can't hear you?"

The angels can only hear our words.

For He shall give His angels charge over you, to
keep you in all your ways. In their hands they
shall bear you up, lest you dash your foot against
a stone. Psalm 91:11

I think we need to thank the Roman Catholic Church
for speaking that which is not, as though it were so, ever
since Jesus taught us to pray Matthew 6:9:

Our Father in Heaven,

Hallowed be your name.

Your Kingdom come.

Your will be done

On earth as it is in Heaven. Stop.

What is God's will? He picked up a handful of dirt and
breathed life into it. Then He placed Adam on a pedestal,
in the Garden of Eden. Adam was a naked vegetarian that
didn't have to work.

Then the Lord God took the man and put him
in the Garden of Eden to tend it and keep it.
Genesis 2:15

19

Your will be done.

So when Jesus had received the sour wine, He said, "It is finished!" And bowing His head, He gave up His spirit. John 19:30

It is done!

Just as He chose us in Him before the foundation of the world, that we should be holy and without blame before Him in love, having predestined us to adoption as sons by Jesus Christ to Himself, according to the good pleasure of His will, to the praise of the glory of His grace, by which He made us accepted in the Beloved. Ephesians 1:4

Having made known to us the mystery of His will, according to His good pleasure which He pur-posed in Himself, that in the dispensation of the fullness of the times He might gather together in one all things in Christ, both which are in heaven and which are on earth—in Him. Ephesians 1:9

For as many as are led by the Spirit of God, these are the sons of God. Romans 8:14

...And raised us up together, and made us sit together in the heavenly places in Christ Jesus. Ephesians 2:6

No longer do I call you servants, for a servant does not know what his Master is doing. John 15:15

For you did not receive the spirit of bondage again to fear, but you received the Spirit of adoption by whom we cry out, "Abba, Father." The Spirit Himself bears witness with our spirit that we are children of God, and if children, then heirs—heirs of God and joint heirs with Christ, if indeed we suffer with Him, that we may also be glorified together. Romans 8:15 -17

Examine yourselves as to whether you are in the faith. Test yourselves. Do you not know your-selves, that Jesus Christ is in you?—unless indeed you are disqualified. But I trust that you will know

that we are not disqualified. 2 Corinthians 13:5

Somebody better call down there and tell Bishop T. D. Jakes (at The Potters House) that the Holy Ghost went drill instructor on my behind! I was praying about these things, meditating on the word. "But Lord, I don't know. This doesn't sound right. This isn't the church I grew up in." The Holy Ghost said, "Yes it is, it's the Holy Bible." I said, "But Lord, But..."

WHEN I PICKED UP THAT HANDFUL OF DIRT AND
BREATHED LIFE INTO IT,

DID I NEED TO ASK THE CLAY WHAT I WAS DOING?!

What could I say to that? I knew "no, sir" was insufficient.

I know I'm supposed to say this:

Hear this Clarion call, we are in the latter rain!
Hear this Clarion call, we are in the latter rain!

Now I was turning this over in my head. The latter rain, what's that? I've heard in church sometimes that the latter rain will be greater than the former rain; it will be good when it gets here. So I prayed, well Lord, if we are in the latter rain, when did it start? Then as I was praying, I got to wondering. Did the latter rain begin on the day of Pentecost? Is the Holy Ghost the latter rain which is greater than the former rain of Jesus Christ?

Most assuredly, I say to you, he who believes in Me, the works that I do he will do also; and greater works than these will he do, because I go to My Father. And whatever you ask in My name, that I will do, that the Father may be glorified in the son. If you ask anything in My name, I will do it. John 14:12

Jesus is going to His Father's house; these things and greater will Ken do in Jesus name? Say what? I'm glad.

For God has not given us a spirit of fear, but of power and of love and of a sound mind. 2 Timothy 1:7

I have been crucified with Christ; it is no longer I who live, but Christ lives in me; and the life which I now live in the flesh I live by faith in the Son of God, who loved me and gave Himself for me. Galatians 3:20

I can do all things through Christ who strengthens me. Philippians 4:13

When I was younger, I would ask my mother questions about God or the Bible. She was sharp; she knew most of them, but once in a while I would throw her a curveball. I knew she didn't know this one when I got the generic response:

For now we see in a mirror, dimly, but then face to face. Now I know in part, but then I shall know just as I also am known. 1 Corinthians 13:12

Oh, ok? What is that supposed to mean?

That was thirty-five years ago. Now what do I see when I look in the mirror? I see the Holy Ghost wearing a ME suit! Of course you are going to see the Holy Ghost wearing a YOU suit, you know what I mean.

Recently, during prayer, I was wondering when all this had happened. I don't remember sitting down with my mother and discussing the Bible.

The Holy Ghost said, "It was when your mother was driving you back and forth to Sunday school and vacation Bible school."

AAWWEE MOM!!

Thanks Mom, I love you.

—⟡—

W hat is a sin? A sin is a violation of the law. Fear not, for I have redeemed you. Isaiah 43:1

Worry is the fear that something might go wrong. Do you know any mother that never worries about their children? I'm a father and I worry! Is worrying a sin? If it is, it was forgiven and forgotten at the cross.

He will again have compassion on us, and will subdue our iniquities. You will cast all our sins, into the depth of the sea. Micah 7:19

As far as the east is from the west, So far has He removed our transgressions from us. Psalm 103:12

Now we know that whatever the law says, it says to those who are under the law, that every mouth be stopped, and all the world may become guilty before God. Romans 3:19

...having abolished in His flesh the enmity, that is, the law of commandments contained in ordinances, so as to create in Himself one new man from the two, thus making peace, and that He might reconcile them both to God in one body through the cross, thereby putting to death the enmity. Ephesians 2:15-16

...for Christ is the end of the law for righteousness to everyone who believes. Romans 10:4

But now the righteousness of God apart from the law is being revealed, being witnessed by the law and prophets, even the righteousness of God, through faith in Jesus Christ, to all and on all who believe. For there is no difference; for all have sinned and fall short of the glory of God, being justified freely by His grace through the redemption that is in Christ Jesus. Romans 3:21

Do we then make void the law through faith? Certainly not! On the contrary, we establish the law. Romans 3:31

Do you think that I came to destroy the law or the prophets. I did not come to destroy but to fulfill. For assuredly, I say to you, till heaven and earth pass away, one jot or one tittle will by no means pass from the law till all is fulfilled. Matthew 5:17-18

What then? Shall we sin because we are not under the law but under grace? Certainly not! Do you not know that to whom you present yourselves slaves to obey, you are that one's slaves whom you obey, whether of sin leading to death, or of obedience leading to righteousness? But God be thanked that though you were slaves of sin, yet you obeyed from the heart that form of doctrine to which you were delivered. And having been set free from sin you became slaves of righteousness. Romans 6:15

What is a slave of righteousness?

Is it a king and a priest created in the image of the Most High GOD (Gen. 1:27), saved and redeemed by the blood of the Lamb of God, who was slain before the foundations of the world to pay for the sins of mankind?

> For the wages of sin is death, but the gift of God is eternal life in Christ Jesus our Lord. Romans 6:23

A sin is a violation of the law. We are not under the law; we are under grace. What is a violation of grace? Nothing can separate me from the love of God! Again:

> For I am persuaded that neither death nor life, nor angels nor principalities nor powers, nor things present nor things to come, nor height nor depth, nor any other created thing, shall be able to separate us from the love of God which is in Christ Jesus our Lord. Romans 8:38

So what good does this do me? That all sounds real nice, but how does this help? Why is life this hard?

And war broke out in heaven: Michael and his angels fought with the dragon; and the dragon and his angels fought, but they did not prevail, nor was a place found for them in heaven any longer. So the great dragon was cast out, that serpent of old, the Devil and Satan, who deceives the whole world; he was cast to the earth, and his angels were cast out with him. Revelation 12:7

So the devil and his army of fallen angels are tripping us up. I thought, "Well, at least we have twice as many good angels as bad angels, right?" Hold on! I do not believe the Great God Jehovah settles for anything!

Hebrews 1:14 questions: "Are not all angels ministering spirits sent to serve those who will inherit salvation?"

Who will inherit salvation?

...that if you confess with your mouth the Lord Jesus and believe in your heart that God raised Him from the dead, you will be saved. Romans 10:9

OK. One-third of the angels are rebelling against God and not serving mankind. What do we do?

Then God blessed them and God said to them, "Be fruitful and multiply; fill the earth and subdue it; have dominion over the fish of the sea, over the birds of the air, and over every living thing that moves on the earth." Genesis 1:28

Is a fallen demon or devil a living thing that moves on the earth? Yes, it is! Subdue the devil and rule over all of the angels.

How?

For though we walk in the flesh, we do not war according to the flesh. For the weapons of our warfare are not carnal but mighty in God for pulling down strongholds, casting down arguments and every high thing that exalts itself against the knowledge of God, bringing every thought into captivity to the obedience of Christ, and being ready to punish all disobedience when your obedience is fulfilled. 2 Corinthians 10:3

Therefore submit to God. Resist the devil and he will flee from you. Draw near to God and He will draw near to you. James 4:7

Humble yourselves in the sight of the Lord, and He will lift you up. James 4:10

Indeed we put bits in horses' mouths that they may obey us, and we turn their whole body. Look also at ships; although they are so large and are driven by fierce winds, they are turned by a very small rudder wherever the pilot desires. Even so the tongue is a little member and boasts great things. James 3:3

For the word of God is living and powerful, and sharper than any two-edged sword, piercing even to the division of soul and spirit, and of joints and marrow, and is a discerner of the thoughts and the intents of the heart. Hebrews 4:12

I believe God communicates with us in ways we can understand. So with this vision I will show how God showed us the devil's hole cards (if we were playing cards). This is also a double jump on the checkerboard, or the correct choice in a shell game. Now we all know:

> Yet, you do not have because you do not ask. We are directed to; speak that which is not, as though it were so. James 4:2

> And whatever things you ask in prayer, believing, you will receive. Matthew 21:22

This was always the problem for me, believing when I ask. I know nothing is impossible for God, but will He do this for me? Well, I was groveling in repentance. Begging for forgiveness as usual. Oh, Jesus, I did it again. Please forgive me. "Can you hook a brother up with a lil' somethin', somethin'? You know, if you're not too busy."

You can guess what response I got to prayer. Hello, is there anybody out there?

> Now: I speak that which is not as though it were so!

> Believing, when I ask, that I will receive what I pray!

And therefore, I have __, because I ask __!

A bowl of fruit.

Matthew 7:16 says: " You will know them by their fruits."

I speak these things:

1) I do not have diabetes.

    Many years ago someone told me that they had diabetes. And I remember saying, "Thank God, I don't have diabetes…yet." Does that mean that I am going to get it someday? Approximately eight years ago, the devil shot me with the fiery dart of diabetes. Ok, I've got this one; I started praying. Jesus heal me from diabetes. Jesus heal me from diabetes. Jesus heal me from diabetes. Six years went by; no change. Ok, Lord, I'm about done with this test drive. What am I doing wrong? These things and greater will you do in Jesus' name. After the second trip to the emergency room with blood sugar over 550, I decided to do something different. I stopped eating carbohydrates all together. I eat as much meat and vegetables as I want. In the last eighteen months I have lost forty pounds and feel better than I ever have. That's the good news. The great news is that I haven't taken insulin or pills for diabetes in four months and my blood sugar is just fine. Now someone might say that because of the diet change, my body corrected itself. If that's what they prefer. However I will, celebrate, Jesus, celebrate!!!

2) I do not have gout.

    Several years ago I went to the doctors office for pain in my knee and ankle. Doc said uric acid, which crystallizes in the joints, was pushing the joints apart from the inside. He said this was caused by red meat, seafood and alcohol. That's about all they serve here in Southern Maryland! Ok, I won't eat red meat. Maybe that helped with the weight loss and blood sugar also.

3) I do not have hemorrhoids.

    Self-explanatory.

4) I do have a full head of healthy hair.

I've been bald since I was twenty. Did someone steal my crown? Does it look like I got scalped? I have been speaking this and have much more hair than I did six months ago. I am growing my hair back!

5) I do have intelligent children that do well in school. All five!

The older brother is in the Marine Corps now. He's a sharp young man. He's got skin in the game.

The older sister is working full-time, and is on the Dean's List at college. AT THE SAME TIME! Grandpops is proud of you!

The younger brother just graduated high school and had his college scholarship money DOUBLED! Excellent! As usual.

The only reason the middle sister doesn't get straight A's is because some of them are A+'s. (She needs to bring her grades up!)

And the younger sister is rocking pre-school!

Every day I thank God for, and pray for, all of you.

During a recent Wednesday night Bible study, our pastor's wife, Assistant Pastor Tamera MeBane said, "Knowledge is Power." Now, we've heard this before, but it struck me that night. When we realize who we are in Christ:

I am, created in the image of GOD. Genesis 1:27

I am, a sinner saved by grace. Romans 6:15

I am, a slave to righteousness. Romans 6:18

I am, a prisoner of hope. Zechariah 9:11

I am, another child of God. Romans 8:14

I am, redeemed. Isaiah 43:1

I am, seated in heavenly places. Ephesians 2:6

I am, a member of God's household. Ephesians 2:19

I am, a joint heir with Christ. Romans 8:17

I am, accepted. Ephesians 1:6

I am, an acceptable offering to God. Romans 15:16

I am, anointed to preach the gospel to the poor...and to proclaim the acceptable year of the Lord. Luke 4:18

I am, a King and a Priest! 1 Timothy 6:15 and Revelation 5:10

Last, God said we look like His son Jesus in this suit of righteousness!!

If the supernatural commander-in-chief says we look like His son Jesus in this suit of righteousness, what do you think God's armies of angels are saying? "Oh, yes, Sir! They look like your son Jesus in that suit of righteousness to us, too."

When we "speak that which is not as though it were so", we are prophesying our own future. I used to say things like, "I've never got any money." Or "I just can't find a job." That was right.

Now I say:

I am, healthy, wealthy and joyful.

I am, healthy, whole and well physically.

I have money and more money is coming to me.

Every word that comes out of our mouths is obeyed by the angels. What do you want them to do?

Now is everything going perfectly in my life? Not yet, but I guarantee I've got the devil by the tail this time!

Everyone knows that you don't pick up a snake by the tail, or it will bite you.

In Genesis 3:14, the Lord God said to the serpent:

Because you have done this,

You are cursed more than all cattle,

And more than every beast of the field;

On your belly you shall go,

And you shall eat dust,

All the days of your life.

And I will put enmity

Between you and the woman,

And between your seed and her Seed;

He shall bruise your head,

And you shall bruise His heel.

I hope he doesn't bruise my heel too bad...as I crush his head!

The devil has been beating me like a dog for forty-five years. Does anybody know what I'm talking about? Do I hear the devil asking, WHO LET THE DOGS OUT?!

Every other word out of my mouth is, "Satan, I rebuke you in Jesus' name!" Then I speak good things over what

I'm doing. I will not cut myself shaving. I will not spill this coffee. I will not be late for work. I will not run out of gas. Now I see some storms coming. The third time I can't get the file into the filing cabinet, instead of cussing, I rebuke the devil in Jesus' name. "This file will fit in the drawer, and it will be in the right spot!" I know these are small examples, but this works on everything.

Pastor Bill Winston, in his teaching on "The Law of Confession" talks about life and death, which are in the power of the tongue. We need to speak God's word! Over everything! Over us, our children, our money, our homes, our safety, our joy, our peace. Like Ol' Bill says, our tongue is to our life like a rudder is to a boat (James 3:4). We know a boat can't turn 90 degrees, or a sharp turn to starboard. It takes a while to get the bow to change directions. Believe, when you ask, that you will receive what you pray. Did I believe at first? I have money and more money is coming to me, but my bank account says "$OH NO.00". Pray to God, but row towards shore. I keep speaking these things and am even more encouraged

41

when I see positive results. Things are getting better! We are coming up out of here!

Our Pastor, Dr. Carlton MeBane, said on a recent Sunday, "Send the Holy Ghost in first." He's also who suggested I write this book. I always thought, "look out world, here we come", meaning the Holy Ghost and I. Blessed is he who comes in the name of the Lord. I pray over upcoming situations and then step in at the right time and place. Not always, but:

> Likewise the Spirit also helps in our weaknesses.
> For we do not know what we should pray for as we
> ought, but the Spirit Himself makes intercession
> for us with groanings which cannot be uttered.
> Romans 8:26

Every minute of every day, we are on the front lines of spiritual warfare and every minute of every day we are:

> Yet in all these things we are more than con-
> querors through Him who loves us. Romans 8:37

And He said to them, "I saw Satan fall like light-ning from heaven. Behold, I give you the authority to trample on serpents and scorpions, and over all the power of the enemy, and nothing shall by any means hurt you. Nevertheless do not rejoice in this, that the spirits are subject to you, but rather rejoice because your names are written in heaven." Luke 10:18

REJOICE YOUR NAME IS WRITTEN IN HEAVEN!!!!!!!!!!!!

2 Corinthians 6:2 states:

For He says;

"In the time of my favor I heard you,

And in the day of salvation I have helped you."

Behold now is the time of God's favor, now is the day of salvation.

Salvation is priceless, but favor makes me dance!

I found a new church! I haven't been attending any one church lately; visiting a few, but nothing permanent. The Holy Ghost told me to go to this church. I could tell right away it was spiritual warfare. When my friend at work, Rob Guy, suggested this church, it was confusing. Why couldn't someone, who has been in the same county as I for twenty some-odd years, tell me where this church was? You know, right there. You can't miss it. I knew something was up. I stopped by this church one evening after work. Nobody was there but while I was standing out front praying, "God is this the church?", I looked in the front window and someone had written on the dry erase board, "Welcome to your new church!" Oh ok, God, I hear you now. The first Sunday I attended, the pastor and his wife were out of town. When Elder Harold Bowman welcomed me to the church, it was the usual "where you from", "who do you know." It turned out, he used to rabbit hunt with my babysitter's husband forty years ago. My big momma, Tillie Parker. Is this a small world? Or a big God?

1 Corinthians 2:9 states:

But as it is written:

Eye has not seen, nor ear heard,

Nor have entered into the heart of man

The things which God has prepared for